SCIENCE
in Action
KEEPING HEALTHY

Why do I wash my hands?

Angela Royston

Quarto is the authority on a wide range of topics.

Quarto educates, entertains and enriches the lives of our readers—enthusiasts and lovers of hands-on living.

www.quartoknows.com

First published in the UK in 2016 by
QED Publishing
Part of The Quarto Group
The Old Brewery, 6 Blundell Street,
London, N7 9BH

A catalogue record for this book is available from the British Library.

ISBN 978 1 78493 631 0

Printed and bound in China

Picture credits
(t=top, b=bottom, l=left, r=right, c=centre, fc=front cover)
Alamy Don Smith 16.
Corbis Tom Stewart 20.
Dorling Kindersley Andy Crawford and Steve Gorton 13, 18.
Getty Images Chris Bernard Photography Inc. fc, Loungepark 5l, Jamie Gril 21tl, James Hardy 21b.
Photoshot James Hardy 19l
Shutterstock Larisa Lofitskaya 4, Elena Elisseeva 5r, phdpsx 6b, Suzanne Tucker 7t, Robert Spriggs 7c, Studio_smile 7bl, Lukacs Racz 8l, Robyn Mackenzie 8cl, tamzinm 8cr, Ray Hub 8r, Irina Mos 8b, MaKo-studio 9t, Muriel Lasure 9b, ryby 10, Renata Osinska 11t, Noam Armonn 11b, Kateryna Kon 12t, Nachaphon 12b, Uravid 12–13, ISchmidt 14bl, 3445128471 14br, 3445128471 17t, Juriah Mosin 19r.

Words in **bold** can be found in the glossary on page 22.

Publisher: Maxime Boucknooghe
Editorial Director: Victoria Garrard
Art Director: Miranda Snow
Design and Editorial: Starry Dog Books Ltd
Consultant: Dr Kristina Routh

Contents

Why must I keep clean?

During the day, our hands touch lots of things that make them dirty. We may get sticky fingers from eating, or grubby hands from playing outside.

Getting dirty can be great fun, but we need to clean up afterwards!

Skin also gets sweaty. When we exercise, droplets of **sweat** containing salt and other substances ooze from our skin. This is the body's way of cooling us down.

After a game, football players can end up covered in mud and sweat.

We remove dirt, sweat and germs by washing.

Some dirt contains **germs** – tiny living things that are too small to see. If germs get inside our bodies, they can make us ill, so we need to wash them off our skin.

Amazing skin

Skin stops dirt and germs from getting inside our bodies. It is **waterproof** and stretchy. Most of our skin is covered with fine hairs.

Our skin keeps water out of our bodies when we swim or bathe.

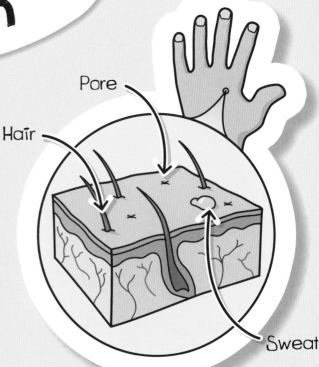

Pore

Hair

Sweat

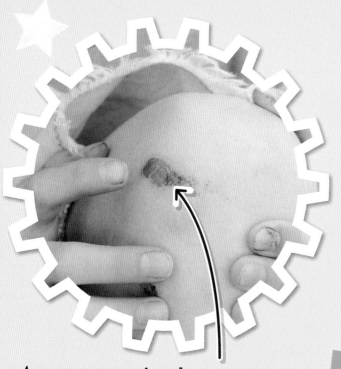

Old skin flakes off and is replaced by new skin. If we cut or scrape our skin, our body repairs the damage and new skin grows over the **wound**.

As a scrape heals, new skin grows under the scab.

Activity

Which of these is most like skin – a piece of cling film, a tissue or a plaster? Which one lets you bend your finger most easily? Which ones are waterproof?

Washing hands

We wash our hands to get rid of dirt. First we wet them and rub them with soap. Then we rinse them with clean water and dry them on a clean towel.

Bubble bath

Nail brush

Flannel

Hand soap

We can use bubble bath, a nail brush, a flannel and soap to keep us clean.

Activity

Try this wash test. Mix some flour and water with your hands to make a sticky dough. Try cleaning it off using cold water. Get your hands sticky again. Now try washing it off with water, soap and a nail brush. Which works best?

If dirt gets stuck under our nails, we clean them with a nail brush. Short nails are less likely to trap dirt than long ones.

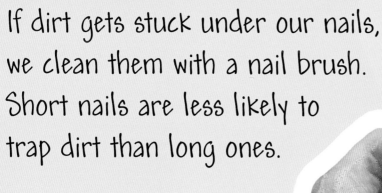

Scrubbing nails with a nail brush is the best way to clean them.

Clean from top to toe

Regular washing in a bath or shower gets all of our skin clean. Skin that isn't washed regularly can become itchy, and feet can start to smell.

After washing your feet, dry the skin between your toes or it may become sore.

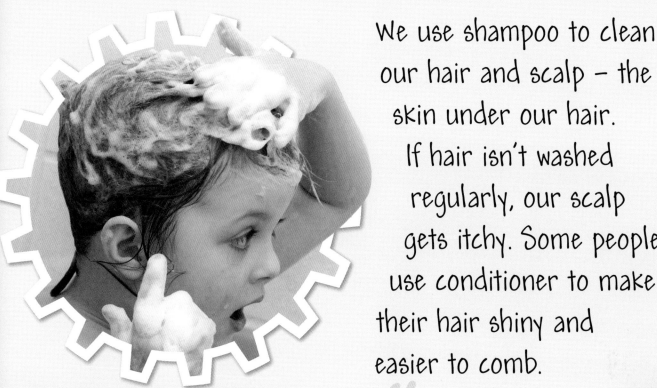

We use shampoo to clean our hair and scalp – the skin under our hair. If hair isn't washed regularly, our scalp gets itchy. Some people use conditioner to make their hair shiny and easier to comb.

We rub shampoo with a little water to make it bubbly. Then we rinse off the bubbles.

Activity

Which brushes out knots more easily – a brush or a wide-toothed comb? Test them out with your friends!

Bacteria and viruses

Bacteria and viruses are different types of germs. Some bacteria are good for our bodies, but others can make us ill.

This is what some bacteria look like when seen through a microscope.

Activity

Cover a glass of milk and leave it in a warm place. After a few days, take the cover off and sniff the milk (but don't taste it). Bacteria in the milk will have multiplied and turned the milk sour.

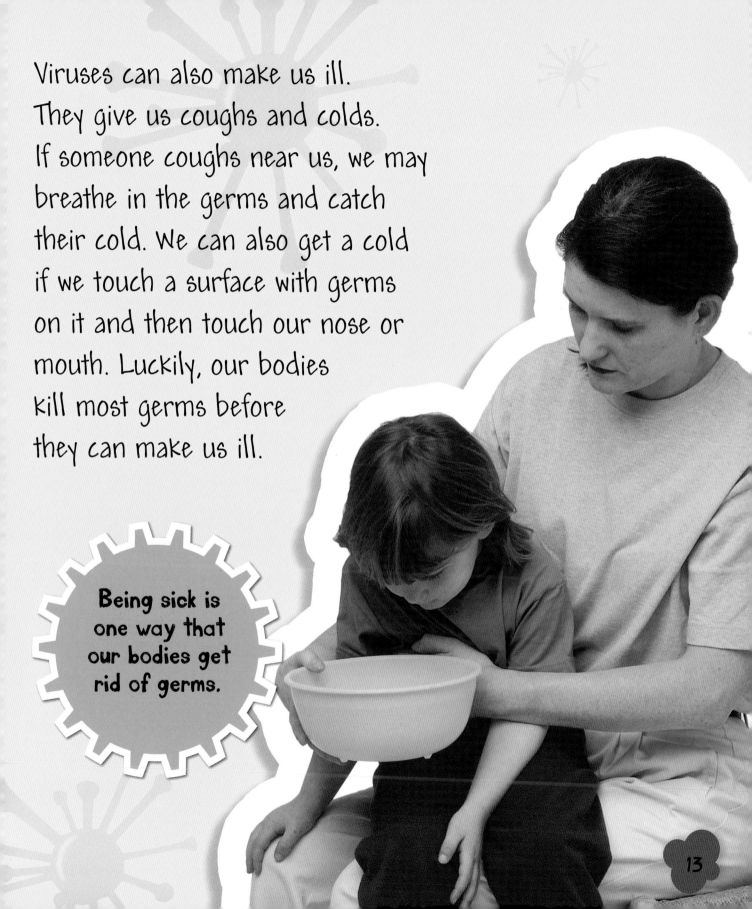

Viruses can also make us ill.
They give us coughs and colds.
If someone coughs near us, we may
breathe in the germs and catch
their cold. We can also get a cold
if we touch a surface with germs
on it and then touch our nose or
mouth. Luckily, our bodies
kill most germs before
they can make us ill.

Being sick is
one way that
our bodies get
rid of germs.

Don't swallow germs

Sometimes germs get into our stomachs. We might get germs on our hands, and then pick up a piece of food. The germs stick to the food and get into our mouths, and then our stomachs.

Germs on our hands can rub off onto our food.

Activity

Have fun helping to wash dishes and pans after a meal. Washing them well will help to get rid of any germs.

The best way to keep germs out of our mouths is to wash our hands before we eat. We should also wash unpeeled fruit before eating it.

1. Germs on fingers can get on to food, and then into the mouth.

2. The germs travel on the food down to the stomach.

3. Acid in the stomach kills most germs.

Some types of bacteria can give us a sore tummy if they get into our stomachs.

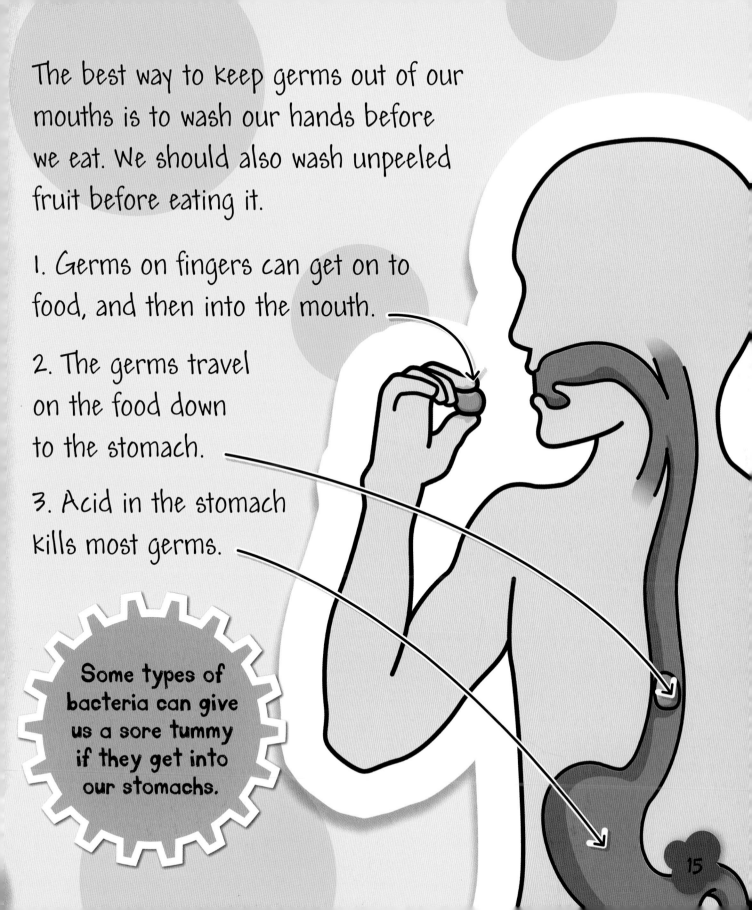

Flush and wash

Poo contains millions of germs. Some of the germs can stick to the surface of the toilet and get onto our hands. That's why we should always wash hands after using the toilet.

Flushing the toilet helps to wash lots of germs down the drain.

If we don't wash our hands, germs from the toilet can move from our hands into our mouths when we eat. These germs can make us sick or give us a bad tummy ache.

Use soap and water to wash your hands well after using the toilet.

Activity

Find out how germs can stick to you. Mix up some powder paint and water. Cover your hands with paint and press them onto a big sheet of paper to make handprints. Germs can cling to your skin just like the paint does!

Don't spread germs

Every time we cough or sneeze, millions of germs shoot into the air. They are carried by tiny water droplets. Other people can easily breathe in these germs.

If you feel a sneeze coming, try to quickly cover your nose and mouth.

When we blow our nose into a tissue, lots of germs can get onto our fingers and stick to anything we touch. After blowing your nose, throw the tissue away and wash your hands.

Activity

If you cough, cover your nose and mouth. Then wash your hands straight away, so that you don't pass on any germs.

Throw your used tissues into a bin.

19

Keeping germs out

When we cut our skin, the blood that comes out of the cut carries germs and dirt away. Washing the cut gets rid of more germs and helps to stop them getting inside us.

You may need an adult to help you wash a cut or graze.

When a cut is clean and dry, we cover it with a plaster to stop any more germs getting in. The wound then begins to heal itself.

A plaster keeps a cut clean until it begins to heal.

Activity

If you graze your skin, keep a diary of what happens to it as it heals. How long does it take for the scab to fall off?

Glossary

Bacteria
Bacteria are a type of germ. Some bacteria can cause illnesses such as ear infections and stomach upsets. Medicines called antibiotics are used to kill harmful bacteria.

Germs
All germs are tiny living things. They are so small that we need a microscope to see them. Germs include bacteria and viruses. They can make us ill if they get inside our bodies. Germs can pass from one person to another.

Viruses
A virus is a type of germ. Viruses cause illnesses such as colds and flu. Antibiotic medicines do not kill viruses.

Sweat
Sweat is the salty water that oozes out through tiny holes in our skin when we are hot.

Waterproof
Something is waterproof when it does not let any water through it.

Wound
A cut or graze that damages our skin.

Index

NEXT STEPS

* Encourage children to take an interest in their own health. Talk about germs and how small they are. Explain why it is important to wash hands, particularly before eating and after using the toilet.

* Talk about why we need to wash fruit and vegetables before we eat them. Ask the children to help you wash grapes, cherries, strawberries and other fruits.

* Encourage children to check the 'use by' dates on food such as yoghurts and smoothies before eating them.

* Encourage children to be aware of food hygiene. For example, explain why it is important to separate uncooked meat from other food in the refrigerator. Explain why we should always wash our hands after touching raw meat.

* Show the children what antibacterial gel is, and explain when we should use it, for example on a picnic when it isn't possible to wash hands before eating.

* Make washing more interesting by collecting a selection of fun soaps in different colours and shapes. Do a 'sniff test' to find out which soaps smell nicest. Bubble bath makes bathing more fun, too.

* Experiment with soap bubbles. Fill a bowl with warm water and add washing-up liquid. Agitate the water to make it foamy. Show the children how to make a bubble by rubbing your thumb against your forefinger and then touching the tip of your thumb to the tip of your finger to make a circle of soapy water. Gently blow on the water to form a bubble. See who can blow the biggest bubble.